Tully Takes Off!

Available in the Tales of Tully series

Tully's Life
This heart-warming story follows the journey of Tully from street dog to much-loved family pet, teaching young readers about the importance of kindness, understanding and hope.

Tully Takes Off!
Tully has arrived in her new home with her new grown-up, but she does not like it one bit! When Tully sees an opportunity to go back to her old life on the streets - the only life she has known up to now - she takes it with both paws. With a search underway, it is up to her new grown-up to work out what Tully needs and help get her safely home.

Tully and the Sad Day
Tully has woken up feeling grey and cloudy inside and she does not know what to do. She cannot help her big feeling because she does not know what it is. As her different feelings begin to work together in the wrong way, it is up to Tully's grown-up to help her to understand what she needs.

Go To Sleep Tully!
It is night time and Tully is tired, but she does not want to go to sleep. Her new grown-up knows that Tully is trying every trick she can to avoid going go to bed! With lots of adventures planned and Tully needing her rest, Tully's grown-up needs to find a way to help Tully learn to not be so worried about bedtime.

Tully and the Midnight Feast
Tully is a newly-adopted dog settling in with her new grown-up. Since her arrival, her snacks have started mysteriously disappearing from the cupboard and appearing under her bed, she seems to have forgotten her manners, and there are days when she just cannot stop eating! Tully and her grown-up need to work together to help Tully with her worries about food.

Tully and the Scary Day
Tully has woken up feeling scared. She isn't really sure why, but today feels like a very scary day, and she just wants to hide. Tully's grown-up is thankfully there to help Tully manage her big feelings and see that the day is not so scary after all.

Don't Touch Tully!
Tully is settling in with her new grown-up. She has learned that the new grown-up is a safe person and she enjoys strokes and cuddles with them. Then Tully starts to meet new people, who want to show her how loved she is. Unfortunately, Tully doesn't feel the same about people she does not know and trust. It is up to Tully's grown-up to find a way to help Tully with her big feelings and to be Tully's voice, when she can't use hers.

Tully and the Tummy Ache
Tully has a tummy ache and it's making her feel quite grumpy. She doesn't want to eat or drink, and she can't get comfortable. Her tummy is sore and it's getting worse! Tully is in a toilet muddle. So, Tully and her grown-up work together to sort the muddle out and help Tully to cure her tummy ache.

Tully's Birthday
It's Tully's birthday, and her grown-up has planned a special day for her, but Tully doesn't feel like celebrating. As the day begins to unfold, so do Tully's big feelings. Tully doesn't know what to do about the big feelings, so she does a bad thing. Luckily, Tully's grown-up is there to help her feel better about herself, and enjoy the rest of her birthday.

Listen, Tully!
Tully does not always like to listen, especially when her grown-up is trying to stop her having fun. Tully decides that instead of listening, she can be in charge. But when things start to go wrong, Tully and her grown-up need to work out how Tully can begin to find listening a little bit easier.

Tully and the Makeover
Tully has been having lots of fun playing in the mud, but now her grown-up says she has to have a bath. Oh dear! Tully is not sure she wants one of those. She is feeling a bit nervous about what is going to happen to her, but Tully's grown-up shows her that there is nothing to worry about. Having a bath is a good thing after all.

Tully and Vera
Tully has moved in with her new grown-up but she is missing her foster carer, Vera. Tully is struggling to understand why she had to leave, and whether it is okay to have big feelings about Vera. It is up to Tully's grown-up to try and help her to understand loss and endings and why, sometimes, they have to happen to make space for new beginnings.

Tully and the Chase
Tully loves to be chased. It gives her a feeling of excitement which starts off as being fun, but one day the excited feeling suddenly and very quickly becomes a feeling which is too big. Instead of feeling excited, Tully starts to feel scared. Tully and her grown-up need to work out how they can play Tully's exciting game without it becoming a bit too much for her, and causing a muddle.

Tully at Christmas
Things are starting to feel a bit different in Tully's house and all around outside. Tully's grown-up looks different, strange lights are appearing everywhere and people have started putting their gardens indoors! Tully is not sure what to make of this thing called Christmas – she just wants everything to stay the same. What can Tully's grown-up do to make Christmas-time a nicer time for both of them?

Tully Goes on Holiday
Tully has gone on a holiday with her grown-up. After a difficult start, things seem to be going well. But when the fairground opens up, with all its flashing lights, loud music and food smells, Tully's big feelings get the better of her, making her want to run. And she does! Tully's grown-up needs to find her in time to show her that holidays can be fun after all.

Tully and the New Rules
Tully likes lots of things about living in a house with her grown-up, but one thing she really doesn't like is all the rules! Tully thinks the rules are all very boring and her grown-up must want to stop her from having fun. One day Tully breaks her least favourite rule, and something bad happens. Tully doesn't know what to do! Can Tully's grown-up get to the bottom of this muddle so it doesn't happen again?

Tully Takes Off!

TALES OF TULLY

Jess van der Hoech

Trauma Tools
& Training

ISBN-13 978-1-83-81987-6-3
Editing by Sarah Ogden
www.jvtraumatools.co.uk

Acknowledgements

As always, to my trusted editor Sarah Ogden for all that you do to make these books come to life. I will never fully know what goes on behind the scenes, but it is a joy to work alongside you on these projects. Thank you.

To the children and families who I meet in my therapy room, from whom I have learned more about hope and healing than any course could ever teach me. Your input, ideas, questions and answers are so valuable to me and I will be forever grateful. Thank you.

To Gemma Pyemont and Emma Gomes from 'Help them Home' who supported us from the moment Tully went missing with much needed advice, reassurance, postering and generally keeping my spirits up! Thank you.

To Christine Walker, Nicki Scriven and the team at Lost Dogs Recovery UK South, who were responsible for getting Tully home safely to me. Nicki knew what Tully was going to do before Tully had even decided what her next move was! I can only hope that one day I will be able to read, predict and understand the children I work with in the same way you do with the dogs you work with. Thank you.

A special thank you to Vera Andric Osmic, founder of the DNV Save Animals charity. Vera builds trust with the street dogs who get to know her as she goes to feed them every day. When the time comes for them to be removed from the street and taken to the safety of the shelter, the 'capture' is force-free, often with Vera simply walking over to the dog, picking them up and putting them in the car! This was how she saved Tully, her puppies and hundreds of other dogs who now live safely all over the world, all down to this wonderful lady and her phenomenal efforts. Thank you.

Preface

This story is based on real-life events that happened after I adopted Tully, an ex-street/shelter dog from Bosnia. Tully was born and lived on the street until she was ten months old, when she was taken into a shelter by Vera, founder of the DNV charity to save street cats and dogs.

For some time, Vera went out to feed Tully on the street, because there was no room for her at the shelter. Aged just ten months herself, Tully had a litter of four puppies. When Vera found Tully hidden with the puppies, she knew she had to bring them to the safety of the shelter as the days and nights got colder in Bosnia. A guard took in one of the puppies and Tully and her remaining three puppies moved into the DNV shelter, where she stayed for two and a half years, until I applied for and was successful in adopting her.

I have owned dogs before and considered myself to be an experienced owner, able to provide Tully with food, warmth, shelter and an abundance of love. In my mind, Tully would come and live in our home, receive all the things she had not received before, be exceptionally grateful, rewarding me with the purest loyalty and love in return. How wrong I was! While I have owned dogs before, I had never owned a street dog. There is a huge difference in the needs and behaviours of a street dog compared to a dog born into a safe, stable and secure environment. As the human caregiver, my needs, behaviour and expectations of Tully were the first thing that had to change. It became apparent to me fairly quickly that I had to provide Tully with the therapeutic care-giving that I have learned about in my role as a therapist working with traumatised children.

When a child has lived with early traumatic experience, it has a huge impact on the brain, body and nervous system, often leading to symptoms which are commonly mis-identified as 'behavioural issues'. This group of children often struggle to regulate emotions; they are unable to self-soothe and experience frequent fight/flight/freeze responses. Adults often react to this with behavioural modification techniques, which simply will not have the desired effect on the traumatised child.

The story of Tully and the questions that follow will enable the adult to begin to understand the physical environment of the child, from the child's perspective. By speaking about Tully, the child using the book will likely be giving the answers that apply to them, allowing the caregiver to explore further and, if necessary, adapt the physical environment or at least become aware of what may potentially be a trigger for the child. This understanding alone can help to begin to create a sense of safety for the child, particularly those who have recently found themselves in a new environment, whether that be a new home, placement, family or education setting.

It is important to understand that when a child moves from one family to another, it can have as much of an impact on them as would be experienced by an adult who moves to a different country. For the adult in this example, every sensory experience will be different; the air, the smell, the food, the water, the culture, the language. The same can be said for the child who moves to a new family in a ten-mile radius. They have to learn to adapt; no mean feat when the process of learning anything can be interrupted by the impact of early trauma. Tully's story can help to develop a common understanding between the carer/parent/adult and child, to help make these difficult transitions easier.

How to use this book

First and foremost, ensure that both you and the child are well-regulated and comfortable when you begin to read Tully's story. Make sure you choose a time when you are unlikely to be interrupted. The child may like a soother, a favourite or fidget toy, a drink or something to suck or chew to help them to stay regulated.

If the child is calm, then begins to try and distract or move away from the reading, make a note of what they have just heard in the text. It is very likely that they will have just provided you with some valuable information about something that they cannot tolerate or want to avoid for now.

The questions have been designed not only to explore the internal world of the child, but to help to develop a common language between the child and adult who are using this book together. The child cannot get the answers to the questions incorrect. Their interpretation of the thoughts and feelings Tully is having may provide some very significant information about the child's own thoughts and feelings. The child may want to expand the answers to talk about themselves and may even be able to make comparisons between Tully's feelings and their own.

Tully Takes Off!

Tully had a new home. A new home and a new grown-up. The new home and the new grown-up both seemed lovely, but Tully did not like it one bit!

Before Tully had moved to her new home, she had been a street dog in Bosnia. This meant that she lived on the street with no one to look after her. Tully had become really good at looking after herself.

When Tully was on the street, she had three puppies to look after too. She had to try and protect them from the other big dogs who also lived on the street. Tully was only small and although she was good at it, this was a very hard job for her.

Can you draw Tully?

How might Tully be feeling living on the street with her puppies?

One day, a kind lady called Vera took Tully and her puppies to a special place called a shelter. This was a place where all the dogs who needed the most help were taken, so they could have food to eat and a kennel to sleep in.

The people at the shelter had a big meeting. They needed to find a grown-up who could take care of Tully forever. They searched and searched and finally, they found Tully a new home, far away in the UK.

Can you draw the shelter?

What might Tully have liked about the shelter?

Would there have been anything she did not like about the shelter?

Tully travelled on a bus for three days and two nights until she arrived in the UK at the new grown-up's house. Tully had never lived in a house before, or eaten out of a bowl, or had a grown-up who wanted to give her cuddles all the time.

Some people on the streets in Bosnia had given Tully and her body big hurts and this had made Tully believe that ALL people wanted to hurt her, especially grown-ups. The only person she knew she could trust was Vera. Tully had liked it at the shelter and she wanted to go back there.

How might Tully be feeling about her new house and new grown-up?

What does Tully need to know about her new house and grown-up?

What are the things that might make Tully feel scared about her new grown-up and house?

What are the things that Tully might find safe about her new grown-up and house?

A few days after Tully had moved to the new house, her new grown-up took her to the park so she could see some other dogs and make new friends. Outside of the new house, there were too many new things to see. Too many new things to smell. Big noises that Tully did not know, that were painful to her sensitive ears. It was all too much!

The big feelings made Tully want to run as fast as she could. The new grown-up was holding Tully on a lead, but using all her strength, Tully broke free from the lead. Tully took off!

What big feelings might Tully have had?

What might have given her the big feelings?

She ran as fast as she could. She ran out of the park, through some gardens, across the road and through a field until she found a place to hide. The place Tully found was an old farm that was not being used any more. It had an old barn that Tully could hide in. Tully stayed in her hiding space so the big feelings could go away.

How might Tully be feeling now?

Meanwhile, Tully's new grown-up was trying to find her. The new grown-up had gathered a team of experts who knew about lost dogs and could come and help. The new grown-up had no idea where Tully could be.

How might Tully's grown-up be feeling?

Luckily, some of the people in the team knew just what to do as they had met lots of street dogs before.

"Tully needs something different to other dogs," they said. "Don't call her name as the noise could make her feel more scared. We need to look for her quietly."

What might Tully have thought when she could not hear people looking for her?

Would she have liked this thought or not?

The team of people all split up and went different ways to search for Tully. They looked at their maps and found places they thought Tully might go. They searched and searched, but Tully was really good at hiding.

After a while, the sun started to go down and darkness fell. It started to feel cold. Tully was tired and hungry. She was also completely lost and did not know how to get home. After several hours, Tully finally drifted off to sleep.

Can you draw Tully now?

Morning came and Tully woke up, confused at first. She had been dreaming she was back at the shelter in Bosnia and when she woke up outside, first of all she thought that she was there, with Vera and the other street dogs. As she opened one eye, she saw that she was still in the barn. She was still lost and alone.

Tully started to sniff. She could smell something good. With her nose in the air, Tully started to trace the smell. It was coming from the ground close by. Tully started to sniff harder. She followed her nose until she found it – a piece of sausage!

Tully was so hungry, she ate the sausage quickly and wished she had more. Suddenly, another piece of sausage dropped from the sky and landed just in front of her. Tully's wish had come true!

Would Tully have had any other wishes when she woke up in the morning?

What else might Tully be wishing for?

Tully was so busy eating the pieces of sausage that she did not notice at first that her grown-up was sitting close by, throwing the sausage pieces to her. The grown-up stayed quiet, throwing the sausage and waiting patiently to see if Tully would come over. The grown-up had been told that Tully needed to come by herself or she might run away again, and the grown-up did not want her to do that!

After she had eaten lots of sausage pieces, Tully felt better. She sat and thought. Her grown-up had come to find her and made sure she had food. The grown-up was not doing anything to make Tully think she was in any trouble.

How is Tully feeling about her grown-up?

How is the grown-up letting Tully know she is not in trouble?

Sadly, Tully was still too frightened inside. She really wanted to go to her grown-up but she just did not know how. As all the big feelings came back, Tully ran off again. She ran and ran and hid in another field. As she began to feel calm again, Tully wanted to make a clever plan. She did not even know why she had run away again, it all just felt too much.

What might Tully do now?

What big feelings might have come back before Tully ran off again?

Later that day, Tully made a new plan. As darkness began to fall again, Tully made her way back to the farm she had slept in the night before. She wanted to go while all was quiet.

When she got to the farm, she could smell something tasty. She crinkled her nose and sniffed around. It smelt like burgers and sausages. Tully realised how hungry she had become as she had not eaten all day long.

She followed the smell, her nose close to the ground, the smell getting stronger and stronger. Closer and closer she came to the smell, until finally, there it was. Burgers and sausages just as she thought! Tully began to tuck in.

Suddenly she heard something clang behind her. She turned and looked quickly. The noise she heard was a door closing behind her. She was trapped in a big cage! Oh no! How had this happened?!

How is Tully feeling now?

Tully was panicking, trying to jump out of the cage. Suddenly in the distance she saw some bright lights. There was a van coming towards her. Two grown-ups who Tully had never seen before were making their way to the cage.

"It's okay Tully," the first one said. "Good girl Tully."

Tully wondered how they knew her name. How did they know she was there?

The next voice Tully heard belonged to her grown-up. "It's okay Tully, I am here. We've just moved a little bit too quickly haven't we?" her grown-up said. "Let's go home and start again."

The two grown-ups that Tully didn't know helped her to get into a smaller crate and then lifted her into the back of their van. It seemed that Tully's grown-up had asked them to set the trap to get her home safely.

How does Tully feel about her grown-up asking the experts to set the trap?

When they got to the house, Tully's grown-up put a crate in the kitchen and covered it with some blankets so Tully could hide in there and look out to see what was going on around her. Tully got into her crate and settled down to rest. She stayed in her crate, just watching.

The next morning, and every morning after that, Tully's grown-up came into the kitchen and said "Good morning Tully, it's a beautiful day!" They even said this when it was raining!

Tully's grown-up had wanted to give her lots of big strokes and cuddles, but Tully had not had big strokes and cuddles before and was not sure if she liked it. Tully did like a chin scratch, so the grown-up did that instead.

How can Tully help her grown-up know what she does and does not like?

Tully had not had meal times and snacks when she was a street dog and did not understand that there was lots of food available for her now. Sometimes, Tully hid some of the food from her bowl in her crate to save for when she was hungry later.

Tully was used to eating food that was not so good for her and she enjoyed eating it, but her grown-up wanted her to be healthy.

In the end, Tully had meals that were made of the meats she liked and some healthy vegetables. For snacks, Tully discovered that she loved cheese and looked forward to snack time so she could have some.

Tully thought that trying new foods was a good thing, especially when she found some new foods that she liked!

Can you draw or write some of your favourite foods?

Are there any foods that you really do not like?

As the days went on, Tully started to get used to her new routine in her new house with her grown-up. Tully started to feel more confident. She had started to learn that her grown-up only wanted to take care of her. When Tully knew that her grown-up could take care of her inside of the house, she realised that she would be safe outside of the house with her grown-up too.

The next time they went out, it was quiet. There were no other dogs or people around and Tully could have a proper look and sniff around the park. She even enjoyed it a little bit!

Why was it important for Tully to know that her grown-up could keep her safe in and out of the house?

How do you know when you are feeling safe?

Where do you feel it in your body?

Tully's grown-up started to teach Tully a lot of things that she had not known how to do before, like playing fetch! Tully had never had a ball to play with, but now she had lots of toys and a person to play with too.

Can you draw Tully playing?

What are your favourite things to do or play with?

Lots of things are different in Tully's life now and even though it was scary at first, now, she has decided she quite likes it. Tully does not want to take off anymore, Tully wants to stay put!

How is Tully feeling now?

What are the things that helped Tully to settle into her new house?

What did you like about Tully's story?

Is there anything you did not like about Tully's story?

Afterword

This is the real-life story of when Tully took off, written by Lost Dogs Recovery UK South, who were able to safely catch Tully. Without them, Tully would probably still be on the loose now!

SAFE – TULLY, a scared Bosnian rescue who escaped when leaving home for a walk in rural Dagnall, Bucks, on Sunday 1st October. Having spent two weeks since her arrival decompressing at home, Tully was going for her first walk when she was spooked by a large man and his dog nearby; she Houdini-rolled out of a safety harness and although able to cling on to her initially, her distraught owner had to let go before things escalated. Tully bolted through gardens and away north, towards Whipsnade zoo.

Raising the alarm on Facebook, local helpers jumped in immediately with postering, spreading the "do not chase/approach" message and sharing essential advice in the hope it would allow Tully to calm down and return home. Unfortunately she didn't, and sightings over a couple of days placed her in various fields around the village, as well as crossing back and forth over the busy road. She was approached by a farmer and ran; she saw her owner and ran. Some cameras were put up and CCTV checked, but found nothing. More postering and door-to-door flyers went out.

On Thursday 5th, Tully was seen at 8am on the road near her home. Target camera locations were identified and plans made to bring LDR cameras up from Sussex. A real-time sighting placed her where the cameras were heading so, on arrival, permissions were hastily secured and a trap put out. It was set for a few hours just in case, but with no sign by 11pm the trap was unset.

Tully appeared on camera the following morning; she was very nervous but spent several hours in the quiet farmyard circling and assessing. Extra-high-value food was added and Tully cautiously stretched and ate under the door, but reviewing the footage it was clear she needed a different style of trap.

Worryingly the last clip on Saturday morning was of Tully sprinting across the farmyard. She was clearly running from something off camera. No sightings came for over twenty-four hours so plans to swap the trap were paused. Would she return to the farmyard? After seven days in Dagnall had Tully been spooked one time too many and moved on?

Lovely weather on Sunday saw people out and about; Tully was spotted in other fields and, crucially, by 'our' farmer from his tractor on Sunday morning. So it was back to plan 'trap swap', with arrangements made for Monday.

The large enclosure trap was in place by 6pm on Monday in a more secluded spot at the back of the yard; baited but unset, several cameras were put up to watch. Tully was reported sunbathing south of Dagnall before heading to the farm and finding the new trap at 7:20pm. She was on and off there for hours, then on her tenth visit at 2am she went inside.

Given her skittish nature, and following her show/no-show/show pattern of previous nights, the plan was to watch and wait again on Tuesday, and return to set the trap on Wednesday.

On Tuesday tea-time Tully was seen by her owner trotting in a neighbouring field. She safely crossed to the farm and the trap at 7:20pm. There was still lots of circling, sitting, laying, watching, waiting, whining and stretching but she was definitely feeling braver this time as she ventured inside at 8:30pm, eating well, before going away and coming back numerous times over the night.

The trap was set by 6pm Wednesday and the wait began. She made her first appearance at 7pm for a circuit and a stretch, then a camera notification at 7:40 put us on alert, and at 7:46pm, Tully's tour of Dagnall came to an abrupt end... much to the relief of everybody except for her!

Not very happy to be contained, Tully was a tricky transfer and was visibly looking for any opportunity to bolt; slowly and carefully, taking no risks, she was loaded into a crate and transported safely home. STAY SAFE NOW TULLY.

THANK YOU to everyone who called in sightings; to Gemma and Emma for stopping everyone trying to 'chase and grab', supporting Tully's owner straight away and mobilising to poster; to local landowners for checking their CCTV and allowing permission for cameras to be set up; and finally to the whole family at Norwick Farm for their total support, flexibility and cooperation to get Tully safe.

About the author

Jess van der Hoech is a qualified therapist who has spent the last ten years studying and working with the impact of developmental trauma and, in particular, the assessment and treatment of children and adolescents with complex trauma and dissociation.

As well as supporting birth families, Jess works with looked-after and adopted children and families, using skills in attachment-focused therapy and therapeutic parenting techniques.

Jess is a supervisor, trainer and motivational speaker with a passion for writing therapeutic books that are accessible to children and families to help with the healing process and to increase awareness in the impact of trauma.

Also by Jess van der Hoech

What A Muddle (2016) ISBN 978 18381987 0 1 (Co-authored with Renée Potgieter Marks)
An interactive, practical workbook designed to help children who have difficulties with emotional regulation to begin to understand what is happening in their bodies. A variety of activities throughout the book enable the child to start to explore these ideas through the story of Sam, while gently encouraging them to begin to verbalise their own experiences. Carrying out the physical exercises in the book can promote changes in emotional regulation. The text is written in a child-friendly, gender-neutral style, and is easy to understand for parents, carers and practitioners alike. For children aged 4-12.

These Three Words (2018) ISBN 978 18381987 5 6
Also available as an e-book. A unique therapeutic novel for teenagers with the aim of linking together the feelings, emotions and behaviours connected to anxiety, with some of the therapeutic tools that can be used in order to enable better self-regulation, increased confidence and different ways of thinking. The book is equally valuable to parents of teenagers with anxiety, giving them an insight and understanding into some of the issues that may be affecting their child, and potentially opening up a line of communication and a way forward between parent and teen.

These Three Words: The Journal (2019) ISBN 978 18381987 2 5
A thought-provoking and hands-on workbook, combining a series of practical exercises and tools designed to assist teenagers who are struggling with the symptoms of anxiety. Addressing the anxious responses in both brain and body, this journal provides the reader with the opportunity to discover therapeutic coping techniques and learn how to apply them to their own personal problem areas, before committing to a twenty-eight-day practice to promote good emotional regulation and reduced anxiety. The journal can be used alongside the therapeutic novel These Three Words, or as a standalone workbook, and it is suitable for use by the teenage reader on their own, with a parent, or in a group.

Beastie, Baby and the Brand-New Mummy (2022) ISBN 978 18381987 3 2 and *Beastie, Baby and the Brand-New Daddy (2022) ISBN 978 18381987 4 9*
A therapeutic story that looks at the external signs of pathological dissociation in a child. Dolly's story helps children who have experienced early trauma to begin to understand, in a very simple way, what dissociation is and why it has happened in their internal world. Tools and techniques are included within the story that parents and caregivers can use to assist the child in the first stages of their healing process. Beautiful illustrations on every page enhance the story of Dolly, and help the reader to relate to the events that happen, to notice the methods Dolly has developed to manage her feelings, and to think about what is happening in their own internal world. For children aged 4-12

Printed in Great Britain
by Amazon

62815640R00038